# Taylor's Tiny Tiger

**Buzz Lee**

# Content

# Taylor's Tiny Tiger

Summer school-break had started out great for Taylor. Today had been super! She had just returned home from her ninth birthday party. All of her friends had been there, and it was so much fun. Her delicious cake was made of ice cream. She got several neat gifts. Oh, and the big water balloon fight. She smiled to herself.

She had really soaked Cody well. Cody was her soon-to-be twelve-year-old big brother. They loved and respected each other very much. It showed when they played together.

They often made-up games and played with neighborhood children. Taylor loved being active and creative. Yes, so far, summer has been playing, riding bikes, hoverboarding, camping, drawing, and fishing. But yesterday, the weather changed a bit. The skies had begun to cloud up. Today started out all gloomy. And now, it was raining! She thought to herself. "Summer is not supposed to be like this in Montana." It was day ten of summer break, and Taylor was already getting bored.

Taylor's glum face did not escape Cody's attention. He said, "Hey Tay! Do you want to play a fun video game with me?"

Cody was always playing video games. Taylor really did not like video games that much. She preferred physical activities. Things like bike rides, skating, swimming, and bouncing on the trampoline. She was also very creative, and loved drawing things. After thinking, she answered Cody in a disappointed tone, "No… You always win. I think I will just do some art. Maybe I will draw something."

Cody shook his head no and replied cheerfully, "Ok, but if you change your mind… I will be in the basement."

Taylor's face suddenly lit up with excitement. "I am going to draw! Now, where did Pop-pop put that new art paper and those fancy-colored pencils?' She ran upstairs to her room and stopped. Looking around, she asked herself, 'Now, where did he put those things? Aha! Pop-pop said he would put them in my chest!" And there, at the foot of her bed, was the big cedar chest. She kept her favorite things inside it. As she lifted the somewhat heavy lid, she spied the paper and pencils. They were still all tied up together. She admired the wide beautiful green ribbon and bow. Pop-pop always made any gift seem extra special. This present was for finishing third grade with all A's. She now fully remembered last night. "It was just after Mom had tucked her in bed. Mom and Dad had let Pop-pop come up and wake me; because of his special gift for me. Then he made me, make a promise. Promises are important…"

As Taylor remembered the encounter, she smiled to herself. She was half awake then. Now, what had Pop-pop told  her? Just as he handed her the paper and pencils? Yes. He whispered into my ear, "These are indeed beautiful pencils and fine paper! But… they are magical as well. I traded an expensive gold coin for them.' Then he leaned away, smiling widely. He then grew serious and looked around the room. It was as if he was trying to find something… or someone? He abruptly faced Taylor and whispered in a serious tone, 'The Leprechaun I bought these from… swears they are enchanted. Enough for now; you need to sleep. I will set these inside your chest. Promise me, before you draw anything, you will call me."

Taylor remembered mumbling back, "I promise Pop-pop. Thank you!"

Pop-pop said, "When we talk, I will tell you how they are supposed to work. For now, I will put them here, inside your chest. Remember… call me before you draw." 

Taylor laughed to herself. "That is why I couldn't remember where they were. Pop-pop had put them in the chest…" Her Pop-pop sure had a strange imagination. He was always playing tricks on her and Cody. She took the pencils and paper and ran back down to the kitchen table. She quickly tore off the green ribbon and bow. Tossing it to the side, she picked up a sheet of paper. It really did have a special feel about it. She even thought her fingers had tingled a little bit.

As she sat the paper down, she realized she needed more light. She got up and opened the window shades wide. That helped a little. She still needed more light. Taylor ran back up to her bedroom. She returned quickly with her art lamp. This was her favorite Christmas present ever. Her grandmother, "Manny," had given it to her. Manny always seemed to know just what Taylor and Cody wanted and needed. Taylor plugged the lamp's cord  into a nearby outlet. This lamp was special. It would take any picture placed on top of it, and put it on a blank sheet of paper. It made it a lot easier to draw anything that way. Now, Taylor was a good artist. She liked her drawings to look as real as possible. Taylor paused and thought… "What do I want to draw… A shark!" She began looking through her books and found one. It was a Great White. They grow up to be over twenty feet long and live in the oceans. She placed the picture on top of her lamp. Ahh, it fit. She turned on the lamp… and there it was on the paper.

Taylor hurriedly opened the box and pulled out the black pencil. It felt so good in her hand. It was so perfect for her fingers. When she touched the tip of the pencil to the paper, she was amazed again! It seemed to glide over the paper. It was almost  like… it was drawing the shark and not Taylor. She thought to herself, "Pop-pop was not teasing. These are good pencils." She laid the black pencil down on the table. Then she leaned forward and studied the drawing. As she was leaning, the pencil rolled over beside the drawing at the same time. Taylor was so into the drawing; she did not notice it. Taylor gazed at her lifelike shark and thought, "This shark needs water to look perfect." She was reaching for her blue pencil, when she remembered her art rule. 'You always use one tool at a time. Always put a tool back in its place when you have finished using it. Then when you need it again… you will know exactly where it is!' So, she carefully put the black pencil back inside the box. Then she pulled out the most beautiful blue pencil. It almost seemed to twinkle in her hand.

She began making little blue waves above the shark. But when she started bluing the entire area around the shark… something strange began to happen. The shark actually wiggled! Then it flipped its tail! That was scary on its own. But when some water splashed up into Taylor's face… She screamed… Loud!

Cody came running up the basement stairs. Taylor's mom and dad entered the kitchen right behind him. They stopped at the kitchen table. Taylor was sitting there staring at the paper in front of her. She seemed to have some water on her face and in her hair. Her expression was rather strange. A mixture of wonder and fear. Her dad asked softly, "Honey, what happened? Are you okay?"

Before Taylor could answer her dad, her mom asked, "Honey, how did you get your face wet?"

Cody, seeing she was not injured, began laughing at Taylor's expression. Mom thereby assumed Cody had squirted Taylor, with his water gun. "Cody James! Did you squirt your sister with your water gun? I told you not to do that inside!"

Cody now had a serious look on his face. You did not want Mom mad at you. He pleaded, "No, Mom. I did not squirt her. I was downstairs playing my game. I heard her scream and ran up here to help her."

They all looked back at Taylor with questioning expressions. Taylor said softly, "No, Cody did not squirt me. The shark I drew did…."

Mom, Dad, and Cody all looked at each other questioningly. Then they all moved around behind Taylor. When they saw the shark, they were very impressed. Cody was the first to say anything, "No way! You could not have drawn that shark. It looks like it could swim off of that page!"

Taylor glanced up at Cody with a fearful look and said, "Don't say that! Don't even think that, Cody!"

Taylor's Dad was surprised by Taylor's response to Cody. He put his hand gently on Taylor's shoulder and softly said, "Taylor, calm down. Cody is just very impressed with your artwork. For that matter, I am as well. You need to learn how to respond to a compliment. You must also realize; we all were worried for you. We all hurried in here because you screamed. We all love you. Now… what made you scream?"

Taylor thought for a second, then replied in a soft, timid voice, "I thought my shark moved…."

Her Dad smiled and said tenderly, "Here, let me see it." Taylor carefully lifted up the shark drawing by the paper's edge. Her dad, thought Taylor was holding it that way, so she would not smudge the drawing. So, he held it by the edges as well. He smiled as he admired the shark. Then, with pride in his voice, he said, "This is a beautiful shark, Taylor! I am so impressed. This is your best drawing ever.' He turned the drawing, so Mom could see it too and said, 'What do you think, Sweetheart?"

Mom smiled with pride. As she reached out to hold it, she said, "Taylor, you are so gifted. This is so lifelike. It looks like it could…"

Before mom could finish her sentence, Taylor realized, if the shark's tail could

move… it probably could bite as well! She jumped up and grabbed the drawing out of her daddy's hands. She quickly tore it up into several pieces and pushed them apart, all over the table top.

Everyone was shocked at Taylor's reaction. Mom was the first to speak. She seemed a bit upset, as she said with a hurt voice, "Taylor, why on earth did you do that? We were just complimenting you. I loved that shark. I would have framed it. Sweetheart, if your art gets you this upset… You might need to put it away for today."

Taylor did not mean to hurt anyone's feelings. She feared what the shark might do. Taylor even envisioned the shark jumping off the page and biting Mom. Taylor, though afraid of the shark, really liked that shark as well. Taylor thought to herself, "Why did I tear it up! Am I going crazy? Did that shark really splash me?' She touched her face, and it was dry. Then she touched her shirt. It was dry too! She thought to herself, 'I really do need a break.' She looked up at her mom and said, 'Mom…Dad, can we go out for lunch?"

Mom and Dad looked at each other for a second. Dad winked at Taylor and said, "We can be ready in five minutes. You tell us where you want to go.' He turned to Cody and said, 'Cody! Finish up your game, or pause it. We are going out for lunch!"

Now alone at the table, Taylor carefully picked up the shark drawing pieces. Nothing happened. She cautiously fit them all back together. Suddenly, the pieces started to reattach to each other. Water started leaking from the paper.

Taylor quickly separated the pieces and divided them into two parts. She took one half and dropped them loosely into the kitchen trash bag. Next, she ran outside to the big trash can and threw the

remaining pieces into an empty milk carton. Then she let out a sigh of relief. She was confident the picture pieces could not get back together again. Back inside the house, she cautiously picked up the blue pencil. It seemed normal now. She gently placed it back in its box. She closed the box, then taped the lid down.

She took the paper and straightened the whole stack. Now all of the edges were nice and even. She placed the stack, in a paper-sized plastic storage box. Satisfied the art supplies were secure, Taylor carried them upstairs to her room. When she opened the

chest, both boxes began to vibrate in her hands. She hurriedly laid them down in the chest. Then she closed the lid as fast as she could. She had no idea what might happen next.

Cody walked by her room and saw her staring at her chest. He sneaked over behind her. Then he grabbed her arms and shouted, "Got Ya!" That is when the fight started.

# A Startling Discovery

The next morning Taylor was lying in her bed. She was still deep in sleep when suddenly her eyes popped open wide. She sat up and carefully looked around her room. She gave out a relaxed sigh. For some reason, she had dreamt a giant shark was swimming after her. She believed, it might have been trying to eat her! Are those pencils really magical? Did that fish really splash water on her? She abruptly sat up in bed. Why did she tear it up? Yikes! She had to put that drawing back together. If indeed it was real, her mom and dad needed to see it splash. Taylor's mind was racing.

Just then, she heard a mechanical roar outside the house. She ran to the window. It was the garbage truck! And their trash can was next to the curb. The lid was open. That meant it was empty! Oh no! Now the truck was driving away. Well… she still had the paper in the kitchen. She  jumped up and ran down the stairs. When she opened the kitchen garbage can… it was empty as well. Cody never emptied all the trash cans like he was supposed to. Just then, Cody walked in from the garage.

He smiled and said cheerfully, "Good morning, Tay. I thought you were sleeping in?"

Taylor was upset. Cody could hear the disappointment in her voice as she answered him, "Why did you pick today; to empty all the trash cans?"

Cody looked down on Taylor with a questioning look, "I don't know why. Something just woke me up, and I really wanted to do it. It is my chore, you know."

Taylor knew Cody was right and said laughingly, "Mom and Dad are going to fall over in disbelief!"

Cody smiled, but then frowned and said, "Hey! I did what I was supposed to do. They will be happy."

Just then, their mom and dad walked into the kitchen, still in their pajamas. Dad said, "What is going on? You two are not fighting again, are you?"

Taylor was quick to answer, "No, Dad, we are not fighting."

Mom smiled and said, "Good. Cody, I see you have emptied all the waste cans inside." She glanced out the kitchen window and said, "But did you get the big trash can to the curb in time?"

Cody smiled, "Yes, ma'am! It is even back from out front."

Dad said, "Good job Cody! How about some breakfast, guys?" Dad was a real breakfast king. Everything he made was delicious. Cody and Taylor both smiled and nodded yes eagerly. "Well, I can make some waffles… with whip cream and fresh strawberries? I can even make some bacon and eggs if you like?"

Mom, Taylor, and Cody all excitedly said, "Yes!"

Mom said, "Why don't you two go upstairs and get dressed while dad fixes breakfast." With that, they ran upstairs and changed out of their pajamas.

They were busy all day, including a long hike up and down a mountain. That afternoon, an exhausted Taylor walked into her bedroom. She slowly walked over and plopped face down on her yellow bean bag chair. She was sighing deeply when she heard a soft rattling noise. She turned her head toward the sound. It was coming from her cedar chest. She slowly got up onto her feet. Now when she stared directly at the chest, the noise stopped. She stood frozen in place for ten long seconds.

Nothing happened. Finally, she relaxed and turned her head away from the chest. Immediately the chest rattled, even louder than before! Taylor flinched back in disbelief. What could be in there making that noise? A rattlesnake? A racoon? The Shark?! As she cautiously approached the chest, the rattle quieted down. She paused and glanced over her shoulder and around the room. She did not want that Cody sneaking up and scaring her again. He was not there. She had even closed her door this time. She faced the chest. Then she bent forward and extended her reach as far as she could. She slowly raised the near side of the lid. She was leaning her head to the side, to see inside better.

There were no dark animal eyes staring back at her. Slowly, she fully opened the lid and then locked it in place. There was no rattlesnake there. It was the pencils that were

rattling. Cautiously she reached down and gently touched the trembling box. That very instant, the rattling stopped. Taylor thought to herself… "I wonder… What would it do, if I removed my hand?" Slowly, she lifted her hand off of the box. Nothing. It was all quiet. Taylor relaxed. She thought to herself, "Now why would that thing rattle like crazy before, and not now? Well… I really don't feel like drawing anyway."

She reached for the lid's latch. The pencil box began to rattle, even louder than before. Taylor recoiled back at the sound. After a few seconds, she reached in again. This time she picked the box up. It stopped rattling, but it was softly shaking in her hand. She pulled the tape off the lid. It vibrated faster and even tickled her hand. She pulled her fingers away from the lid, and the vibrating almost stopped. Taylor knew now, that the box wanted her to hold it. What else did it want? When she thought out loud, "I wonder if it wants paper!" The box became still. Taylor said, "Ah… So… it is paper that you want!" Taylor bent over, picking up her paper. It was then, from behind her, she heard a familiar but ominous voice say, "Ah ha... So… it is paper you want...."

She quickly pulled the pencils and paper to her chest. Then Taylor stood straight up and faced… Cody. She yelled out, "Cody, don't sneak up behind me like that!"

It just happened that mom was in the hallway. She had seen Cody sneak into Taylor's room. Mom had followed Cody. And now she had an, "I am not pleased" frown on her face. She said sternly, "Cody James! (That is Cody's middle name. You are always in trouble, when parents use your middle name.) I saw you sneaking in here. Through a closed door, I might add. You have disrespected Taylor's privacy. On top of that, you tried to scare her. Well, mister! You will stop doing that to your sister! I better not hear of it again. Do you understand me?"

Cody had been caught in the act. He knew he could not explain his way out of this. So, he lowered his head and said, "Yes, Ma'am…' Then he turned to Taylor and said, 'Sorry, Taylor…"

Mom folded her arms and said, "And…"

Cody mouthed his words carefully, with a hint of sincerity, "And… I will do my best to never do that to you again." That seemed to appease mom.

Taylor was equally tactful. Not wanting to stir up her mother's ire toward her. Taylor softly said, "It is ok, Cody. I will try to not tease you as well."

Cody hugged Taylor, then quietly left the room. Mom remained, looking down at Taylor. She felt that she needed to talk some with Taylor, "What are you doing, Honey?"

Taylor was now perplexed. She did not want to tell her mom about the box's rattling. She was afraid if she did… Mom might take the pencils away. So, she carefully said, "I… was just thinking… I might try to draw some today."

Mom appeared to be happy with that, "I think that would be wonderful, Taylor. Your work is getting so lifelike. I was really impressed with that shark.' She paused, as if in thought, then said, 'I do want to see your future work. I treasure all of your art. So, before you tear something up, let me see it. Okay?"

Taylor was relieved. This was not much to ask of her. She smiled and said, "I will, Momma."

Mom smiled and gave Taylor a hug. Then she said, "Tay, you were very sweet with Cody. You know, that he teases you, because he loves you. He just has to learn, what is acceptable, and when to do it."

Taylor nodded in agreement. Her mom smiled and left the room. Taylor sighed. She was all alone again… except for the now vibrating pencil box and paper.

# A Tiger by The Tail

Taylor closed her door softly, then walked over to her desk. She sat the boxes down, then then turned on the desk light. The paper box began to shake. But when Taylor sat down in her chair, the shaking stopped. She took out a sheet of paper, then the pencils started to shake. Taylor said out loud, "Boy, you guys really like this paper." She picked up the pencil box and opened the lid, then sat it down on the desk. She thought out loud…" Let's see… I think I will start off with…" Before she finished her thought, the black pencil started to slide up slowly. Taylor's eyes locked on to the pencil. When it cleared the box top, it floated over to Taylor's open right hand. Taylor's mouth was open in amazement. With her left hand, she adjusted the paper on her desk. She realized; she didn't have her copy lamp. But she was confident. She felt she could draw anything with these pencils.

She thought to herself… "What to draw… I know… a Bengal Tiger cub!" The big smile on her face faded fast. For the pencil between her fingers was moving! The pencil was pulling Taylor's hand toward the paper! Suddenly… in an instant… Taylor became one with the pencil. She was getting into it. Within seconds she had sketched out the form of a tiger cub.

Every place on a tiger that
needed black was black.
Then the pencil box started
to rattle. Taylor relaxed her
hold on the black pencil. It
floated up and away towards
the box. Just as the black
pencil left her fingertips, a
golden orange pencil rose up
out of the box. As the

pencils approached each other, the tops leaned in toward
each other. As they passed, they tapped their top ends
together. That resulted in a bright, a beautiful rainbow burst
of sparks, shooting out of their ends, for a few inches. As the
black one slid into the box, the orange one eased into
Taylor's waiting fingers. Taylor smiled widely and said, "Let's
do this!" Her hand was flying over the page. She was filling
in the orange next to all of the black. Which looked very
furlike. The white was already there with the color of the
paper. It was time to do the eyes. Tigers usually had golden
brown eyes. Sometimes even very rare greenish ones. Taylor
was growing to trust these pencils. "What color should we
use for the eyes?" She released her grip on the orange one.
Sure, enough, it floated up toward the box as another rose
up out of the box. There was that sparkly tap. Now the new
pencil was firmly in her fingers. It was an awesome honey
golden-colored tool. Eyes are very hard to draw, but this was
quick. The little tiger's mouth was open. Taylor needed to
color the tongue and gums. With that thought, there went

the pencils all by themselves. This reddish-pink one was perfect. Taylor smiled and said, "Perfect! Or, should I say 'purr-fect'." She laughed out loud. She was really having fun. Minutes later, the tiger was finished. Taylor could not believe her eyes. She thought out loud, "This is a wonderfully life-like tiger." She was admiring it; when her eyes were drawn to its tail. Did she see it move! She thought she saw the tail twitch. She closed her eyes and shook her head. She stared at the tail carefully. Nothing. Then about ten seconds later, it twitched! This time it moved a lot more than before. Then the tiger swung its tail back and forth widely. It looked up at Taylor! Its tail was getting thick and round. It was even coming up, just off the page!

Suddenly, the reddish-pink pencil flew out of Taylor's fingers and into the box. The box closed itself as well. Taylor did not know what to think. The tiger's tail was starting to swing around, and up higher out of the paper. Taylor slowly picked up the paper. She reached over and caught the tail with her fingers. She pulled on it softly, away from the page. There was a little resistance, then out popped the tiger cub. It landed on its feet in the middle of her desktop. It was well over twice the size of the one she drew. It was just a bit bigger than a large house cat! It was beautiful and had such soft fur. Yes, she was not afraid to pet a baby tiger… should she be? Taylor was crazy happy. The tiger seemed to like Taylor too. It rubbed its head on Taylor's hand. Then her arm, her face, and it purred too!

# When a Cat is a Cat

A thousand thoughts raced through Taylor's mind. "Oh! How beautiful! Will mom and dad let me keep it? If not, where can I hide it? Do I need to hide it? Will it grow? Will it eat and drink? Uh oh… will it pee and poop!" She decided to just love it for now. She thought out loud, "I need to name you. You, beautiful ball of fur! But… what? Cuddles… no. Paige, because you came off the page. That was clever, but it wasn't right. The cub leaned over and licked her hand. It made Taylor jump. That tongue was like wet sandpaper! Suddenly Taylor knew the cub's name, Sandy. She said it out loud, "Sandy!" The cub responded to the name. Sandy jumped down to the floor and began to explore the bedroom. Taylor watched her new love with awe. Then Sandy saw himself in Taylor's wall-mounted dressing mirror. Sandy backed away carefully, until he was clear of the cat in the mirror. Then he cautiously peered around the chest and saw himself again. Taylor chuckled at Sandy's reactions. She walked over to Sandy, picked him up and held him in her arms. Taylor was falling deeper in love with this beautiful creation. She showed Sandy the mirror again. Seeing himself in Taylor's arms helped him a lot. Sandy seemed to understand and licked Taylor's cheek. Taylor sat Sandy down on the floor. He bounced over to the mirror and put his paw on his reflection. Then he scampered back to Taylor, and they played for an hour or so. Sandy was a curious little rascal.

Taylor suddenly came back to reality. It was Mom's voice. She was calling her downstairs to dinner. "Oh no,' Taylor thought.

'What am going I to do with Sandy? I can't just leave him… alone in my room.' She looked at Sandy's sharp little teeth and claws. Then she looked into Sandy's eyes and said, 'I better put you inside my chest. Don't you worry. I will be back for you as fast as I can." With that, she carefully placed Sandy inside the chest. He fussed a bit at first. She could hear him moving around scratching. Then he was quiet. Taylor slowly turned, closed the door behind her. Mom called for her again, and Taylor shouted back, "Coming, Mom!"

Nothing much happened at dinner. There was some conversation about Taylor's drawing last night. Taylor's mom said, "Tay, I was talking to Pop-pop and Manny earlier. Pop-pop said you really need to talk with him about the pencils. He said you would understand… Tay, is there something special about that set of pencils? Or, is Pop-pop just wanting to hear your voice again?" … Mom was waiting for an answer.

Taylor felt like she couldn't tell her mom about the pencils. Not right now, anyway. Taylor thought, "She would go crazy if she knew Sandy was upstairs. It would be best to talk to Pop-pop first. He is the one who gave me those pencils."

Taylor smiled at Mom and said, "I really do need to thank Pop-pop for that gift again. They are very high quality. I had no idea how good they were until I used them yesterday.' She paused and studied her mom's reaction. Mom seemed to be good with Taylor's response. Taylor continued, "Are they at home? If they are, I will call him right after dinner."

Taylor's response did satisfy her mother. Mom said, "That would be a very nice thing for you to do. When you and Pop-pop finish talking, call me over. I need to talk to him and Manny about summer plans." Dinner conversations shifted to what books were being read and summer camps.

Just then… there was a loud thud from upstairs. Everyone jumped. They all stared upstairs toward the noise. Taylor's mind raced, "Had Sandy gotten out of the chest!?" She looked at Dad questioningly, then Mom. Mom asked Taylor, with a knowing look, "Taylor? Did you leave your book on the window sill edge again?' Taylor's room had a window seat; where she would often lay on a cushion and read. She often fell asleep there. Then her book would fall onto the floor with a thud. It was a good cover for Sandy jumping around... for the moment.

Taylor said, "I might have left it on the edge of the

pad… I will run up and put it on my desk. Then I will call Pop-pop. Ok?"

Her Dad spoke up, "Don't worry about that book falling, Tay. I like to hear that thud. It tells me that you have been reading. Reading…." Taylor knew the rest of the sentence.

Cody and Taylor both chimed in, in a sing-song way, finishing Dad's sentence, "You are getting smarter and prepared for life!" Dad was a big reader. He always wanted Cody and Taylor to read. So, whenever he said "Reading…" Cody and Taylor always finished his sentence for him.

Dad chuckled and said, "Go get that book, Tay!"

Taylor slowly opened her bedroom door. Her book was indeed on the floor. But it was not by itself. Sandy was there sniffing and pawing it. Taylor quietly closed her door and said with a whisper, "You! You rascal! How did you get out of the chest…? It does not matter.' Then she thought about the book. She remembered placing it on the floor. So, if the book didn't fall, what made the noise? Taylor said out loud, 'The chest lid! You crawled out, didn't you?' Sandy was over next to her and rubbing himself on her legs. 'Oh, you are a clever fellow, aren't you? But, if I put you in that chest, you need to stay in that chest.' Taylor thought for a second. 'What if he couldn't breathe in there… Maybe he crawled out for air! Wait a minute.' She looked at the chest. The chest lid was up. Who opened it? She walked over and looked inside. As she stared down inside it, Sandy jumped over and into the chest. He began to paw and lick the pencil box. Taylor thought, 'Why are you licking that box… Oh my goodness! Are you thirsty or hungry?"

Sandy looked up at her and "Mewed" like a thirsty tiger cub would. Then he picked up the box with his teeth and sat down at Taylor's feet.

Taylor took the pencils from his teeth and said, "Ahhh… you are thirsty and want me to draw some water or tiger's milk?" At the mention of tiger milk, Sandy "Mewed" again. Taylor ran over to her desk. She didn't give it another thought. At once, the pencil box opened, and out flew the black pencil to her fingers. Then from the chest flew a sheet of paper. It settled down on the desktop right in front of her. Soon a nice bowl took shape. The pencils were trading themselves out quickly. Soon a beautiful tiger pattern was all around the outside of the bowl. Taylor pressed her fingers onto the bowl and pulled it right out of the page. It was a very large bowl. It would hold maybe a gallon. The pencils were back in action. Taylor was now drawing a colorful pitcher. It was full of milk. Taylor assumed it was tiger milk. She pulled on the handle. Out popped a huge pitcher. It was full to the brim. Sandy was getting excited. He probably could smell it, as he was pawing on Taylor's leg. Taylor said, "Okay. You will get some. But no messes!" She poured about a quart of the milk into the bowl. Then she carefully sat it down in front of Sandy. He sniffed it. He rubbed his head on Taylor's legs and purred. Then he returned to the bowl and lapped up every last drop.

Taylor smiled as she looked down at Sandy. She thought to herself, "Sandy, you are nothing but a big kitty… I wonder if you will grow? Would Mom and Dad let me keep you? How do I tell them how you got here?" Taylor knew it was going to be difficult to explain. She realized Sandy might want some more milk. So, she poured him another quart-sized serving. Sandy lapped up all of it. Then he jumped up on the bean bag chair, curled up, and was asleep. He was so cute and beautiful at the same time… Taylor picked up Sandy and gently laid him down inside the chest. She gently closed the lid and stepped back. Taylor realized she needed to talk to Pop-pop badly. She was excited yet fearful for Sandy. She had no idea what might happen next with this tiger. She sneaked out the door and ran downstairs to call Pop-pop.

# O o p s !

Pop-Pop answered the phone, "This is the Pop-pop! What troubled little girl calls at this time of the day?"

Taylor giggled and said, "Pop-pop, you are so silly. But I do really need to talk to you… about the coloring pencils you gave me…"

Pop-pop spoke up with some concern in his voice, "Tay… you haven't been drawing, have you? I told you to talk to me first!"

Taylor was sad and embarrassed. Why had she not done, what her dear Pop-pop had asked her to do. So, she apologized. "Yes, Pop-pop. I did draw some things, and I realized that was wrong. I should have done as you asked me. There is no excuse for what I have done. I just need to know, how to make things right, between you and me first. Then we need to talk about the drawings,"

Pop-pop blurted out, "Drawings! How many have you done? What did you draw?"

Taylor felt bad that she had let her Pop-pop down. She was tearing up and sheepishly asked, "Can you forgive me first?"

Pop-pop's voice was soft and loving this time, "Yes, sweetie. I forgive you. Don't be sad, remember we love each other. We both made mistakes here. I should have waited until you were fully awake. I should have explained it all to you in the morning. I just wanted you to get them on your birthday, so don't feel bad. I will now explain the good and bad, that can happen with the beautiful paper and pencils."

Taylor could hear the sadness in his voice. She realized just how much Pop-pop cared for and loved her, Cody, Mom and Dad. She said, "Aww… Pop-pop, you are such a good grandpa. I am sorry for not doing what you asked me to do. I really had no idea that these pencils and paper were really magical…."

Pop-pop spoke up excitedly, "Are they really? I did not know, if that little fellow was lying or not. I could see that the paper and pencils were of fine quality… When he told me the rules of drawing with them, I just thought he was just trying to close the sale…"

Taylor interrupted excitedly, "Pop-pop, they are truly magical!" She was still worried about the shark. Not to mention the tiger cub upstairs… that she hoped was still asleep and not into mischief.

Pop-pop responded with excitement, "They are! Well, I'll be a monkey's uncle! I am glad to hear that! I gave that little fellow my Chinese gold piece for them...' Pop-pop realized if drawings were actually magical... then the rules he received from the little man were very important. 'Taylor... what have you drawn?"

Taylor recounted the shark drawing in detail. Pop-pop was concerned. Then he asked, if that was all. Taylor then told him about Sandy. She finished by saying, "Pop-pop, he is so cute. I love him so much."

Pop-pop said carefully and sincerely, "Taylor... if the rules for these drawings are factual... and at this point, I think they are. We must follow them. We also must make the best of any mistakes we have made."

Taylor agreed, "Yes, Pop-pop, but what do we need to do? What are the rules?"

Pop-pop drew in a deep breath. "Well, for starters, do not feed Sandy anything real. He must only eat what you draw. Once you feed him anything from this world, he will become a real animal. He will quickly grow into a large dangerous tiger. You say you have drawn and fed him milk. Keep giving him the milk you have drawn; and he will be fine. Draw him a nice jungle to live in. After you play with him, put him in the jungle drawing. He will like that, and you can always bring him out."

This pleased Taylor. She said, "That is what I will do, Pop-pop."

Pop-pop replied, "Taylor, Manny and I will come right over. I will write down the other rules… as best I can remember them."

Taylor was so relieved she said excitedly, "Okay, Pop-pop! When you get here, come up to my room. Mom, Dad and Cody do not know about Sandy. They really don't understand about the shark either. I didn't want to try to tell them about this, until we talked."

Pop-pop said, "Ahhh, yes. I understand… I have some explaining to do as well. We will have to get them all together; and fill them in on what is happening…"

Taylor agreed. Having Pop-pop and Manny with her, will really help in clearing this all up. She knew, that she should not keep things, from her Mom and Dad. Cody… not so much. She smiled and said, "Thank you, Pop-pop! Love you so much! See you soon!"

Pop-pop chuckled and said, "Love you, Tay Tay… and I can't wait to see Sandy!"

# He's Watching You!

Taylor gave her mom's cell phone back to her. With a "Thank you, Mom… Oh! Pop-pop and Manny are coming over for a quick visit."

Mom cocked her head and asked, "Why are they coming here now? We will see them tomorrow… Did they say why? Are they staying for dinner?"

Taylor said in a cheerful tone, "Mom, they just want to talk about the art supplies Pop-pop gave me on my birthday. Excuse me, Momma. I need to hurry upstairs and get them all together."

Taylor turned and ran up the stairs. She heard her mom say, "Why didn't they call us… oh well, the message is received. No bother.' Then she called out to Taylor's dad, "Honey! Pop-pop and Manny are on their way over for a short visit!' He replied with a questioning, "Ok…?"

Taylor opened her door quickly and stepped into her room. Unknown to her, Cody was lurking behind the door. As she closed the door behind her… He sprang towards her back side with a roar… in an attack pose. His knees were bent. His hands were up by his face. His fingers were all curled imitating claws. His mouth was open, showing his teeth!

Unbeknownst to Cody, his every move had been tracked. From over inside the chest… A certain small but adequate tiger, was stalking him! The lid of the chest was raised open a crack. It was just enough for those honey gold eyes to see all.

Sandy knew, by instinct, that this intruder was a predator! This evil-doer had set himself in a hiding place. There right beside Taylor's trail. Sandy could only suppose that this creature meant harm to his Taylor. So, when he heard Taylor's footsteps coming… (Yes! He already recognized her steps. Remember… she feeds him and plays with him.) Sandy crouched down. He was ready to take care of this would-be attacker.

Just as Cody was in the middle of his growl. And when Taylor began hollering. Sandy had leaped up and out of the chest. Roaring as only a small tiger can. In just two hops, he leaped and grabbed Cody. Sandy wrapped his forepaws around Cody's right thigh. The next instant, his teeth grabbed Cody's bottom. Sandy's claws and teeth had not drawn any blood…yet. Cody looked down on his attacker… his eyes were like saucers! He started to reach for Sandy. Sandy gave out an ominous growl and flexed his teeth and claws. Cody got the idea instantly, that this was not a bright idea. He cried to Taylor, "Tay, please get him off me!

Taylor reached out and stroked Sandy, saying with lullaby tone, "That's my big tiger! Sandy is the best friend in the world. Come to Taylor, sweetie. I have some yummy tiger milk for you!"

As Sandy relaxed his grip and yielded to Taylor's loving touch… Cody rubbed his eyes in disbelief. He blurted out…" Taylor! Where did that cat come from? He is so cool. He looks just like a tiger! Wow!' Cody paused then asked pointedly, 'Mom and Dad don't know about him, do they?"

Taylor shook her head no and said, "And don't say a word either."

Cody cocked his head. Then with a little sass in his voice said, "Taylor… Mom and Dad both have special senses. They will know about your new pet, in just a few minutes…"

Taylor quipped back, "I know."

Cody was taken aback by this response. He then asked, "Are you going to tell them you brought this cat home… And have been hiding it from them in your room. Ha, boy, are you in trouble. I am glad I am not you…' Cody was thinking… Then he excitedly asked, 'Has Ranger seen him!" Ranger was the family's dog, a yellow Labrador Retriever.

Taylor was still holding Sandy close to her and loving him. And Sandy was doing the same. She said, "No, I haven't done that yet." She carefully locked the bedroom door. Then set Sandy softly down on the floor.

Cody was admiring Sandy. "That is the most incredible cat I have ever seen, Taylor. I understand why you want him. But you have to tell Mom and Dad. Where do you hide him?"

Taylor said with a sigh, "Cody… You are not going to believe this…" Cody looked down at her with a serious face. Then she said, "I drew Sandy, and he came to life."

Cody laughed loudly… "You almost had me…" He looked at her, and she was stone-cold serious. "Do you really believe you did that, Taylor?" Cody was concerned, because that never happens in real life. He was thinking his sister was … losing her understanding of reality.

Taylor said glibly, "Well, Manny and Pop-pop will be here in a minute or two, and we will be having a family discussion about Sandy and more. For now, since you have met Sandy… Do not under any circumstances give him real water or food. Bad things could happen." She could see that look on Cody's face again. "Pop-pop will explain it all, Cody. I know I am just your little sister and don't know that much about life…"

Cody had heard that tone before. He knew she had been insulted. She was obviously not crazy. Now he was getting excited again. "Do you think Sandy would play with me?"

Taylor was relieved, and could see Cody was warming up to Sandy. She said, "Sure, just sit down and call him over. Stick out your hand and let him see you are not a threat. Pet him, and you will be playing with him in no time." And just like that, Cody and Sandy became friends. Time passes quickly when you play. There was a knock on Taylor's door, followed by "Taylor, its Pop-pop! Can I come inside?"

Taylor jumped up off the chest and opened the door. Pop-pop peeked around the opening door. When he saw Sandy, he gasped and said, "He is beautiful, Taylor…"

Cody responded, "Why, thank you, Pop-pop. You don't look bad yourself!"

Pop-pop chuckled and said, "Taylor, I am so excited for you. Have you made him that jungle drawing yet?"

Taylor said, "Close the door, and I will do it in a flash." As Pop-pop closed the door, Taylor opened the chest. The pencils began to rattle, and the paper began to move. When Taylor sat down at her desk, she looked back at the chest and said, "Come pencils and one sheet of paper!"

Cody really thought Taylor was crazy at this point. But when the pencils floated past his face, and the paper followed them. Cody's expression was one of awe and disbelief. The box opened, and the black pencil floated right to Taylor's hand. Pop-pop looked at Cody and said, "Now watch the artist work, big brother!"

Cody kept rubbing his eyes! Taylor was rapidly sketching out a jungle scene. Then the black pencil floated towards the box as the green pencil approached it. Then they touched ends and they sparkled. As the black pencil slid into the box, the green one slipped into Taylor's hand. Sandy could see the activity above. Curiosity got the best of him. He leaped up on top of the desk. He pawed at the green pencil. That set the pencil into faster action. Seconds later, the paper looked like a lush jungle. Sandy stuck his paw down into the paper.

At this, Cody yelled out, "No way!" This resulted in Sandy jumping back and falling off the desk.

Taylor glared at Cody and said sternly, "Cody, you frightened Sandy! The drawing is not ready yet. You hold him while I finish…"

Cody looked up at Pop-pop. Pop-pop said, "For now, Cody, do as she asks." He smiled and winked at Cody. Cody bent down and picked up Sandy. Cradling Sandy in his arms seemed to relax Cody. That was, until Sandy became fascinated with the buttons on Cody's shirt. When Sandy decided to bite the pocket button… well, he managed to get some of Cody as well. That's when the dance started. Cody was clutching Sandy, trying not drop him. Sandy apparently thought this was some new play. So, he bit the button again… with similar results.

Pop-pop reasoned, it would be better for him to hold Sandy. When he got his hands around Sandy, the cat went limp. Pop-pop took Sandy into his arms; and Cody gave a huge sigh of relief. Sandy looked up at Pop-pop and pawed his cheek softly.

Then he studied Pop-pop's shirt looking for buttons. Pop-pop grinned and said, "You will find no buttons on this T-shirt, you rascal."

By this time, the green pencil seemed to know it was finished. Out of Taylor's hand, it arose. Then it floated towards its box home. It was greeted by the brown pencil as it passed. There were more sparkles, which fascinated Cody. Once in Taylor's fingers, all sorts of creatures began to appear. There were monkeys, birds and rabbits! Then all of the pencils all took their turns in Taylor's fingers. The blue pencil was last. As it finished, a beautiful clear blue stream flowed through this paradise on paper.

Cody excitedly begged, "Let me draw something, Taylor!"

Pop-pop entered the conversation at this point, "I think we have more important things to do right now, Cody. Later on, if Taylor is willing, that will be fine.' He paused and looked down at Sandy. 'We have a furry issue here, that we need to take care of. Taylor, take Sandy… and let him see the drawing. If he wants to go in, let him."

Cody was staring at Pop-pop like Pop-pop had lost his mind. Taylor carefully took Sandy and let him look the drawing over. When he put his paw into it, he pulled it back quickly. He looked back at Taylor and licked her cheek. Then he jumped down into the jungle below. In seconds he disappeared into the undergrowth.

Taylor had tears in her eyes as she looked up at her Pop-pop. She cried softly, "Will I ever see Sandy again, Pop-pop?"

Pop-pop hugged her and said, "I think, whenever you really want to see him, he will be there. But Taylor, you must never reach into the paper. It might be able to pull you into it. I do not know if you could ever be pulled out."

Taylor was thinking to herself and asked Pop-pop, "Can anybody reach into the paper Pop-pop?"

He looked sternly at her and said, "Taylor, don't even think about reaching into the paper. It is another dimension. We have no idea what is in there. Anything you can imagine might be in there… as well as things you don't know about." He paused and studied her face. "Should I take these pencils and papers, so you will not be tempted?"

Taylor had a horrified expression, "No! They are mine! You cannot take back a gift!"

Pop-pop studied her face and said, "Taylor, I think I might have given you something, much more powerful than I thought. These are very strong tools. Note, I said tools… not toys. You have great responsibilities with these tools. And the tools can take over your every thought. You must remember… You are the master over them. If you cross over into the paper…'

Taylor finished for him, "They become master over you?"

Pop-pop smiled and said, "Well… let us just say… the magic ends."

Taylor shrieked, "You mean if I reach inside the paper, I cannot draw like this again?"

Pop-pop nodded  and said, "Maybe."

Taylor added, "What about Sandy! I will still have him… right?"

Pop-pop shook his head no.

That settled it for her. Then Pop-pop looked at Cody and said, "I do not know what would happen if anyone else did this, Cody. So, you two need to keep this a secret between the two of you. Cody, these were a gift to your sister. I expect you to honor her ownership of these tools. You could even harm your sister, if you ever used them. Promise me you will not use the pencils, or tell any of your friends." Then he looked down at Taylor, "And you must do the same, Taylor. No one other than Cody and your parents needs to know anything about these items. Am I understood?"

Both Cody and Taylor mumbled out, "Yes, Pop-pop. We will keep this a secret."

Pop-pop smiled and said, "Good! I would never want anything to happen to either of you. So… should an emergency arise… what do you do?"

Cody and Taylor responded with a "Y—E—S Pop-pop. We would call for Mom, Dad and you."

Pop-pop smiled and said softly, "Taylor, slowly turn and look at Sandy."

Both Cody and Taylor turned to see Sandy. He was back on top of the desk, and pawing at the jungle drawing. Then he reached down into the water. It looked like he was trying to catch a fish! When he pulled his paw back out, water dripped off it, and onto the desk.

Cody screeched, "N-O Way!" as he reached out and touched Sandy's wet paw.

Taylor picked up Sandy and cradled him in her arms. As he began to purr, she asked him, "Sandy, if I let you go into this beautiful jungle… Will you come visit when I call for you?' Sandy took both his paws and wrapped them around Taylor's head. Then he pulled her head close and began licking her face. She gently pulled him off her face and said, 'I will take that, as a yes." She sat him down in front of the paper. He looked down and studied the drawing. All at once, he looked at Taylor and made a "Meroww" sound.  Then he dived into the paper. It was like watching television. Sandy was romping all around as birds flew off and monkeys ran amok. Then Sandy jumped into the clear stream after a fish. Water splashed out and got all over Cody, Taylor and Pop-pop. When they had stopped laughing, out of the page sprang Sandy. He brought a visitor with him. It was that fish. Which he promptly gobbled up, right in front of them.

As they were chatting about how neat it was… Their excitement was doused as they heard from behind them, "My, my, what an unusual cat! He looks just like a tiger! Taylor! Pop-pop… you guys, have some explaining to do here…" Yes… it was Mom. She had heard the commotion coming from the room and had to investigate.

Cody, Taylor and Pop-pop stood there and looked at each other. Cody shrugged his shoulders and lifted his hands up in the air with an "I don't know anything" face.

Taylor said with an understanding tone, "Mom… why don't you sit here, on my chest. This is going to take a while."

After much disbelief and some demonstrations, Mom said cautiously, "Pop-pop! You should have told us (Mom and Dad) about this gift. This could be very dangerous to everyone. What if she had drawn a poisonous snake!' She jumped to her feet. 'Taylor, please tell me you didn't draw a snake!"

Taylor gave Cody an impish glance. Cody knew what she meant and gave her a smile and nod. Taylor said, "Oh, Mom, don't worry, he doesn't have any teeth…"

Mom screamed, "Where is it! Did it go back into the paper?" Cody and Taylor both stared down at the chest that Mom was standing by. Mom looked down and saw Taylor's black belt end sticking out of the chest. It was right by her leg. When she first saw it, she jumped back away from the would-be snake. At which, Cody, Taylor and Pop-pop had a good laugh. Mom did not see any humor in that, but smiled and said, "So, you haven't drawn anything even resembling a snake?"

Taylor shook her head 'no' and said, "Relax, Mom, here is all I have drawn." Then she showed her mom all she had done. With the exception of the shark… But Mom did not seem to be too concerned with it anyway. She was all over Sandy. Sandy seemed to like her as well. So, they all thought, because he was pawing at Mom's apron pocket.

Mom smiled and said as she reached into her pocket, "oh, you're a precious little kitty!' She pulled out a cookie! And was starting to hand it to Sandy, saying, "I bet you would like this nice cookie…" As Sandy was sniffing the cookie, Taylor

lurched forward and grabbed the cookie. She had it all. As she was looking for any crumbs; Mom said, "Taylor, I was trying to bond with Sandy! I have other cookies for you and Cody." At this point, Pop-pop explained Taylor's actions. How any earthly food would turn this kitten into a real tiger. Mom started shaking her head no in disbelief. Then she stood up straight and said, 'Ok, I need more schooling on these magic pencils. And, I want it now." So, Pop-pop went into all the details he knew. As he talked, Sandy was rubbing on Mom's leg and purring. Then he sneaked his paw up to her apron pocket. Mom covered it with her hand and stayed focused on Pop-pop. When all of her questions were answered, she finally seemed satisfied.

Taylor asked her, "Mom can I keep Sandy! You don't have to buy him any food. He will go into the paper every night. I guess that is where he poos and tinkles. But if he does have an accident, I will clean it up."

 Mom could see how Taylor loved Sandy. But she asked, "why didn't you tell me about this yesterday?'

Taylor looked down and away from Mom and said, "I was afraid. That you and Dad wouldn't understand. That you all wouldn't let me keep Sandy."

Mom felt sad for Taylor, "Oh Taylor… I am so sorry you felt that way. You need to know, your daddy and I would never do anything to hurt you. I hope you understand, we will need Daddy to approve you keeping Sandy…' Taylor had been feeling better listening to Mom. Then she realized, there was more to do. She would also have to fill her dad in on all of this. Mom saw her expression and said, 'Tay, do not worry.

You have the best Daddy in the world. He would give you the moon if you wanted it. So, let's get Sandy and go see him now."

Taylor hoped Mom was right, but she was already feeling better. She realized now her secrets were a burden. She was happy to get rid of them.

Dad was very interested in Sandy and the pencils. He wanted to see the tiger bowl and see Sandy have some drawn-up milk! Taylor brought down the bowl, the paper with the pitcher and the pencils. Dad was amazed at the floating pencils. But when Taylor poured the milk into the bowl… He stood up and said, "Oh my goodness!" Sandy was so hungry, he gulped the entire bowl down.

Dad agreed it was safe for Taylor to keep Sandy. However, he warned Cody and Taylor sternly to never go into the paper. This was way too dangerous. He also made Taylor and Cody promise, to never tell anyone of the pencils or Sandy. They promised. Dad also made Pop-pop promise to tell him and Mom everything, about any future gifts before buying them.

Manny said, "I told him. I thought these were dangerous. But you know Pop-pop… He is just a big kid. These pencils screamed out to his imagination. He couldn't help himself. I promise, I will keep him in line from now on." At that, everyone laughed, even Manny. It was the close, of a somewhat tense evening.

# Down in the Dumps

The next morning Taylor found Sandy in her bed! He was on her chest, breathing in her face. When she opened her eyes… He licked her face. The scratchy tongue by itself was bad. Then he immediately began snuggling her neck! That made her squirm and break out laughing. That encouraged Sandy to snuggle more. Taylor was laughing so loud, that it brought Mom and Dad into her room. That did not stop Sandy or Taylor. They were both up on the bed and bouncing like crazy.

It was Mom that stopped the fun. She said in a firm voice, "Taylor! You know you should not be bouncing on the bed!" Taylor immediately stopped. Sandy bounced again, not wanting the fun to stop. Then Mom said in a firm voice again, "Sandy! That means you as well." Sandy scooted around behind Taylor's legs! Then he peeked out from in-between her knees. He looked afraid and so pitiful. That made Mom break into a giggle. Then she said, as she approached Taylor and Sandy, "You two were raising the roof in here. I am surprised the neighbors are not over here, ringing the doorbell!" Then, as she reached out to pat Sandy's head… The doorbell did ring!

Cody yelled from downstairs, "I will get it! – It's Pop-pop and Manny! Do you want them to come up?"

Mom walked out to the stairs landing and said, "You guys didn't have enough of us yesterday? Well, the coffee is in the pot. You know where the cups are. We will be down in a minute. I have batter for waffles in the bowl. Manny, if you want, you can start a batch…"

Manny was cheerful, "We will be down here, and the waffles are in the iron."

Dad smiled at Taylor and said, "I am sure Sandy is getting tired of this room. Why don't you bring him downstairs… But only if you can keep him from eating anything!"

Taylor thought out loud, "I can make him some tiger milk. That should fill him up. And he can drink it as we eat breakfast!"

Dad was quick to respond, "Wait! No, you don't. He cannot be around real food. We cannot afford to feed a full-grown tiger. Taylor the neighbors would not sit still, for a grown tiger pet in the area. We are willing to keep Sandy as a small tiger. We cannot let you have a full-grown one. Do you understand?"

Taylor nodded and said softly, "Yes, Daddy, I do. And I am so glad you and Mom are going to let me keep Sandy."

Dad said, "You will need to draw food and feed Sandy, if you want to keep him. You better get started, if you don't want to eat cold waffles." At that, Taylor opened the chest and pulled out the paper with the picture of milk. She grabbed the tiger print bowl and began filling it. Sandy was down on the floor in an instant. He was hungry, too. He lapped up a bowl full and wanted more. When he finished the second bowl, he licked his lips. Then he jumped up on Taylor's bed and went right to sleep.

Dad had been watching it all. He smiled and said, "Tay I am going down stairs for my waffle! Make sure he is secure. We are going to have to be really careful with people food around here."

Taylor said "Yes Sir." She thought to herself, "Well, he needs a nap. He has probably been up all-night crouching over me. He patiently waited for my eyes to open. Then like the tiger he is, he pounced on me!" She giggled and admired her tiny tiger. He was so cute and fun. Then she turned and ran downstairs for her waffle.

After breakfast, everyone went into the family room next to the kitchen dining area. Mom said, "Hey, we need to clean up!"

Dad answered, "Aww, get a cup of coffee and sit with us for a while. We will all pitch in and clean it up with you, in five minutes. Ok?"

Mom agreed to that and joined the rest of them. She sat down next to Dad on their couch. The adults were relaxing, sipping their coffee and talking about Sandy. They all jumped when they heard a plate crash to the floor behind them. Sandy had sneaked downstairs and jumped up on the table. His landing was a slider. In the process, he knocked a plate and glass to the floor. Everyone knew without turning who it was. Ranger, the family dog, came bounding through the doggie door from outside. He started barking at Sandy. Sandy was calm and seemed to be curious about Ranger. That was good, because Sandy was not interested in the food all around him.  In a very short space of time, everyone was off the couch and at the table. On the way, Mom had screeched out, "Watch out for broken glass!"

Dad yelled, "Keep Sandy away from the leftovers!"

Cody was yelling for Ranger to be quiet and sit. Taylor ran to Sandy and scooped him up in her arms. Sandy did not seem to be afraid of Ranger. In fact, he was curious about him. He stretched out a leg and pawed at Ranger. Taylor could see that Ranger was just as curious about Sandy. She said, "Cody take Ranger over to the couch. I will bring Sandy, and we can introduce them properly."

Taylor sat on one side with Sandy. Cody on the other end, with his hand wrapped around Ranger's collar. After a few minutes, Ranger calmed down, relaxed and quit his whimpering. He started sniffing the air toward Sandy. Sandy was watching Ranger's every move. Then Taylor could see he wanted to interact with Ranger. She loosened her hold, and Sandy moved slowly toward Ranger. Taylor said, "Cody, hold on to Ranger. Sandy wants to meet him. He will be calm. You need to keep Ranger calm. So, Cody patted Ranger and scratched him behind his ears. This was Ranger's weakness. He loved the human scratching. His tongue was hanging out as Sandy leaned forward and sniffed his nose. Ranger pulled his tongue in and sniffed Sandy. In a few minutes, they were playing chase, which Mom stopped abruptly. Ranger and

Sandy ran over to her and started rubbing on her legs. She said loudly, "You two are going to be a handful."

Then she bent over and petted both of them. 'Taylor! Cody! You need to keep these two calm. We still have some cleaning to do. Put Ranger in the back yard or in the garage for a while." That did not work so well, as Ranger howled and scratched the door. That went on for several minutes. After the kitchen and the dining table were clean, Mom allowed Ranger back inside. After a while, they all settled back down on the couch. Dad  said, "Let's see what is happening on the local news." The TV came on, and the weather forecaster said it was going to be bad for fishing.

Dad was grumbling about the weather, when the news anchors suddenly came on the screen. Excitedly they blurted out, "We have a report from Centerville Waste Management, that is unbelievable! It seems as though someone has put a full-grown Great White shark in the trash! No one can explain it. According to witnesses, this twenty-two-foot-long monster has been eating trash and growing quickly….' At this point, everyone in the room stared at each other with jaws agape. Then they all erupted into laughter. Dad said, 'It will be a long time before they figure this out!' Then he turned to Taylor and said, 'Young lady, there will be no more sharks!"

Taylor smiled and said, "There is one in the bathtub upstairs!"

Mom shrieked, "No!"

Cody said, "I want to see!"

Pop-pop smiled and said laughingly, "She is pulling your legs. Aren't you Tay?"

Taylor smiled and said to everyone, "Got ya! Except for Pop-Pop."

**The End.... Or is it??**